The Little Book of PARKING TICKETS

This book is dedicated
to the tickets we hate and the
bastards who write them.

The Little Book of
PARKING TICKETS

I was only
parked
there
for a
minute.

Let that
be a
lesson
to you

STEVEN APPLEBY
& GEORGE MOLE

PORTRAIT

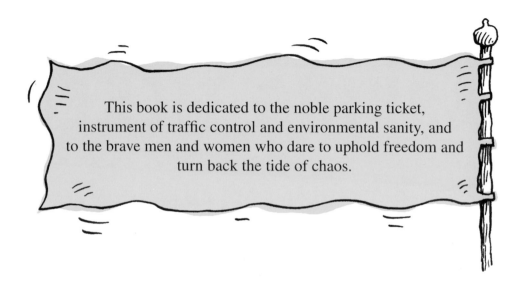

This book is dedicated to the noble parking ticket,
instrument of traffic control and environmental sanity, and
to the brave men and women who dare to uphold freedom and
turn back the tide of chaos.

Place this book on your dashboard or passenger seat, open to this page. Guaranteed to get you off at least one (1) parking control notice.

Visit the Portrait website!

. . . .

Portrait publishes a wide range of non-fiction, including biography, history, science, music, popular culture and sport.

Visit our website to:

- read descriptions of our popular titles
- buy our books over the internet
- take advantage of our special offers
- enter our monthly competition
- learn more about your favourite Portrait authors

VISIT OUR WEBSITE AT: www.portraitbooks.com

CONTENTS

INTRODUCTION: PARKING & ITS DISCONTENTS

Parking tickets are a serious threat to your mental, physical and social health. Experts have shown that receiving a parking ticket has the same deadly effect on the body as a heart attack. These medical renderings show the exact sequence of events:

APPROACHING
THE CAR

OBSERVING
PARKING
TICKET

READING TICKET

DIGESTING INFORMATION

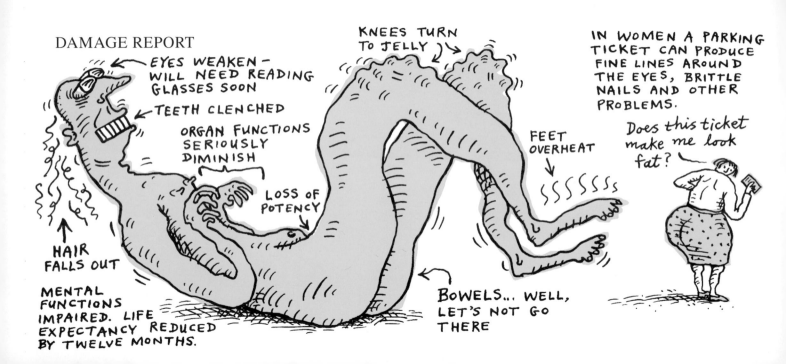

Why do parking tickets provoke such a reaction of rage? After all, a parking ticket is just a little piece of paper slipped under our windscreen wiper by a parking warden, just a notice of violation, an attempt to control traffic congestion, a means of raising revenue from the average citizen, yet another unlawful tax, another attack on human freedom, ANOTHER MEANS OF COVERT GOVERNMENTAL TERRORISM, ANOTHER VICIOUS ASSAULT ON THE COMMON MAN PERPETRATED BY SOME COWARDLY, FASCIST TOOL OF OPPRESSION... BASTARDS!

RIP! SHRED! TEAR!

MR MOLE ENCOUNTERS A TICKET

STAMP!

11

A WORD FROM THE EXPERTS

The Hon. R.C. Fowlton (QC ret'd) writes:
"The parking ticket represents the most unfair of taxes. What right does the state have to demand rent for a portion of the public thoroughfare? A right of way conveys certain rights, one of which is to leave a vehicle while one conducts one's business, such as the purchase of fine French wines or a new chartreuse evening gown, without some vulgar little tin-pot tyrant sticking a grubby scrap of paper on one's nice new car.
Besides, I was only in the shop for five minutes at the most."

Dr Jenny Thalia (psychiatrist) feels that the parking ticket affects us so deeply because it is a wake-up call: "One day the Grim Reaper will stick life's PCN on the windscreen of your soul. A parking control notice is a reminder of mortality, a *memento mori*.* It is a notice of your frailty, your lack of power in the face of authority and your inability to read a simple notice and look at your watch. It can also be a subconscious rebellion against authority and a flouting of regulations. You may secretly *want* a notice of your violation."

**A reminder of mortality*. Dr Thalia suggested we put in this patronizing footnote just so she can show off.

Remember, we're all going to die...

and how does that make you feel?

Dr Thalia suggests that a parking ticket can be viewed as a healthy expression of dialogue between authority and the individual or as a bloody nuisance to decent hardworking professionals who only have one parking spot at their clinic. As a mental health professional she suggests looking at the parking ticket as an opportunity:

- A chance to focus on the good things in life. Maintain your perspective.
- A reminder to be more "present", more "aware". Enjoy the Now.
- An excuse for a good, loud scream. Express your emotions in a healthy way.
- A good motivation to buy yourself a treat. How about a big cream bun? Or a new pair of earrings?

- An excellent reason to ask your doctor for prescription drugs or indulge in unusual sexual activity with a close personal friend.

The Reverend Len Brookings, vicar of North Fetcham, sees a spiritual component: "A parking notice is a reminder that Someone is watching over us at all times. A PCN is a Commandment to render unto Caesar his thirteen pieces of silver. We must try to think of parking wardens not so much as instruments of Satan sent to torment us, but rather as Wingèd Angels bringing good tidings. Except for that Godless Little Shit who slapped one on my Mini outside St Stephens. He deserves to roast in everlasting torment."

Clearly the parking ticket is a document that stirs up powerful emotions. We must understand how we arrived at this place in our history.

A POTTED HISTORY OF PARKING TICKETS

PARKING IN THE ANCIENT WORLD

The earliest parking ticket was found on a clay
tablet at the site of ancient Troy. The Greeks
parked a wooden vehicle blocking the main gate
of the city, completely disregarding an overnight
parking sign. The Trojans towed the vehicle inside
the city walls and impounded it. In complete
contravention of local regulations, the Greeks
sacked Troy, killed all the parking wardens and
sold the remaining inhabitants into slavery.*

*The next time you get a parking ticket you could do the same
thing but you have to maintain a very large army.

18

Fragment of a ticket found on site of ancient Troy
along with thousands of other unpaid tickets.

CUT

In the Bible there is no mention of the "No Arking" ticket received by Noah. Fortunately his son Ham forgot to pay as it would have been a huge waste of money since most of the parking administration were drowned. Sadly two wardens were saved along with all the other species.

THE ROMAN EMPIRE

Throughout antiquity parking violation notices inspired great acts of rage. The Roman Senate sent Hannibal a notice for taking elephants over the Alps into a No Jumbo zone (see right).
Hannibal was so incensed he invaded Italy and laid waste to the land with fire and sword. He painted double yellow lines all over Northern Italy so the Roman army was unable to camp anywhere for more than 30 minutes.

ELEPHANTI

INTEDICTI VIII–V*

YOUR ELEPHANT _ _ _ _ _ _ _ _

WAS SEEN AT _ _ _ _ _ _ _

IN PROHIBITED ZONE _ _ _ _ _ _

_ _ _ _ _ _ _ _ _ _ _ _ _ _

YOU MUST PAY 1 (ONE) BAG OF
SOIL (½ A BAG IF PAID BY
TUESDAY). FAILURE TO PAY
WILL RESULT IN DEATH
BY LAYING WASTE.

*ELEPHANTS PROHIBITED
FROM 8 UNTIL 5.

CUT

The Roman Senate was doomed to make the same mistake when they sent Caesar a notice for crossing the Rubicon while the light was red. In a manner curiously reminiscent of Hannibal, Caesar was so incensed that he invaded Italy and laid waste to the land with fire and sword. After parking the legions overnight in Rome, Caesar went to Egypt in search of elephants. He found Cleopatra who had built multi-storey pyramids to park her ancestors on their way to the Underworld. Caesar's rival Parc Anthony teamed up with Cleopatra to build a fleet of Parking Enforcement galleys that would sail the Seven Seas in search of expired meters. Caesar was stabbed in a Toga-Way Zone; Cleopatra was bitten in the barge by an asp after failing to display her placard; Parc Anthony choked on a congestion charge delivered to him by the Greater Roman Parking Triumvirate. Finally the Senate was decriminalized and all parking notices were handled by the Emperor.

Omnis Gallia in tres partes divisa est.*

*TRANS: Gaul only has three parking spaces.

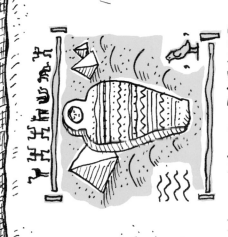

YOU HAVE PARKED
YOUR: GALLEY
SLAVE
DONKEY
CART
CAMEL
HORSE
CHARIOT
ARMY*

*DELETE AS
NECESSARY

IN AN ANNOYING PLACE.
THE PENALTY IS DEATH BY:

STABBING
ASP
BEHEADING
THROAT-CUTTING
BEING BURIED ALIVE*

*ADD MORE AS
NECESSARY

CUT

Several centuries later the Romans did it again. After the Vandals had despoiled their Capitol with graffiti, the Romans sent parking tickets to all the barbarian tribes. The barbarians were so incensed that they invaded Italy and laid waste to the land with fire and sword. Then they set up their own parking laws, renounced their idols and converted to Christianity. Thus, another great empire was destroyed by over-zealous parking enforcement.

During the Dark Ages Vikings roamed the seas burning monasteries and violating parking regulations all over Europe. The Vikings parked with impunity all over the Ancient World, even parking in North America which they called Vinland, after the Vehicle Identification Numbers of their longships.

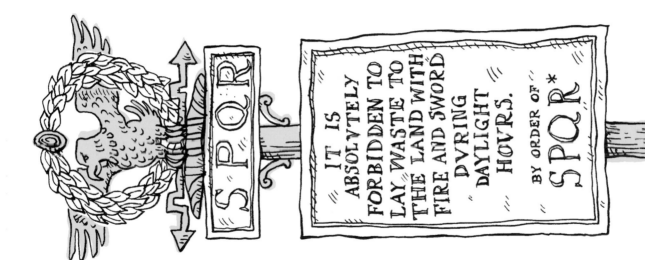

SPQR

IT IS ABSOLVTELY FORBIDDEN TO LAY WASTE TO THE LAND WITH FIRE AND SWORD DVRING DAYLIGHT HOVRS.

BY ORDER OF SPQR*

*Senatorial Parking Quota Restrictions.

CUT

THE MIDDLE AGES TO THE GOLDEN AGE

On to the Middle Ages, when armies frequently parked outside castles with the intention of sacking them. The besieged army would often send heralds with BCNs (Besieging Charge Notices) which they would affix to siege towers and catapults.

EARLY INSPIRATION FOR THE PARKING METER.

CLUCK! CLUCK!

Can you change 2 ducks for a chicken?

These notices infuriated the besiegers who would rush at the castle in a blind rage impaling themselves on parking spikes.

The Renaissance and the Reformation gave birth to the Enlightenment. First, Leonardo Da Vinci invented the parking meter long before anything could actually park at it. Then Martin Luther nailed a Papal Control Notice on a door full of Worms. In an effort to relieve congestion in Paris, Henri Douanier Rousseau published Diderot's *Encyclopedia of Parking Regulation*. Finally, Adam Smith invented the Law of Supply and Demand that proved that if you Supply parking tickets the world would Demand their removal.

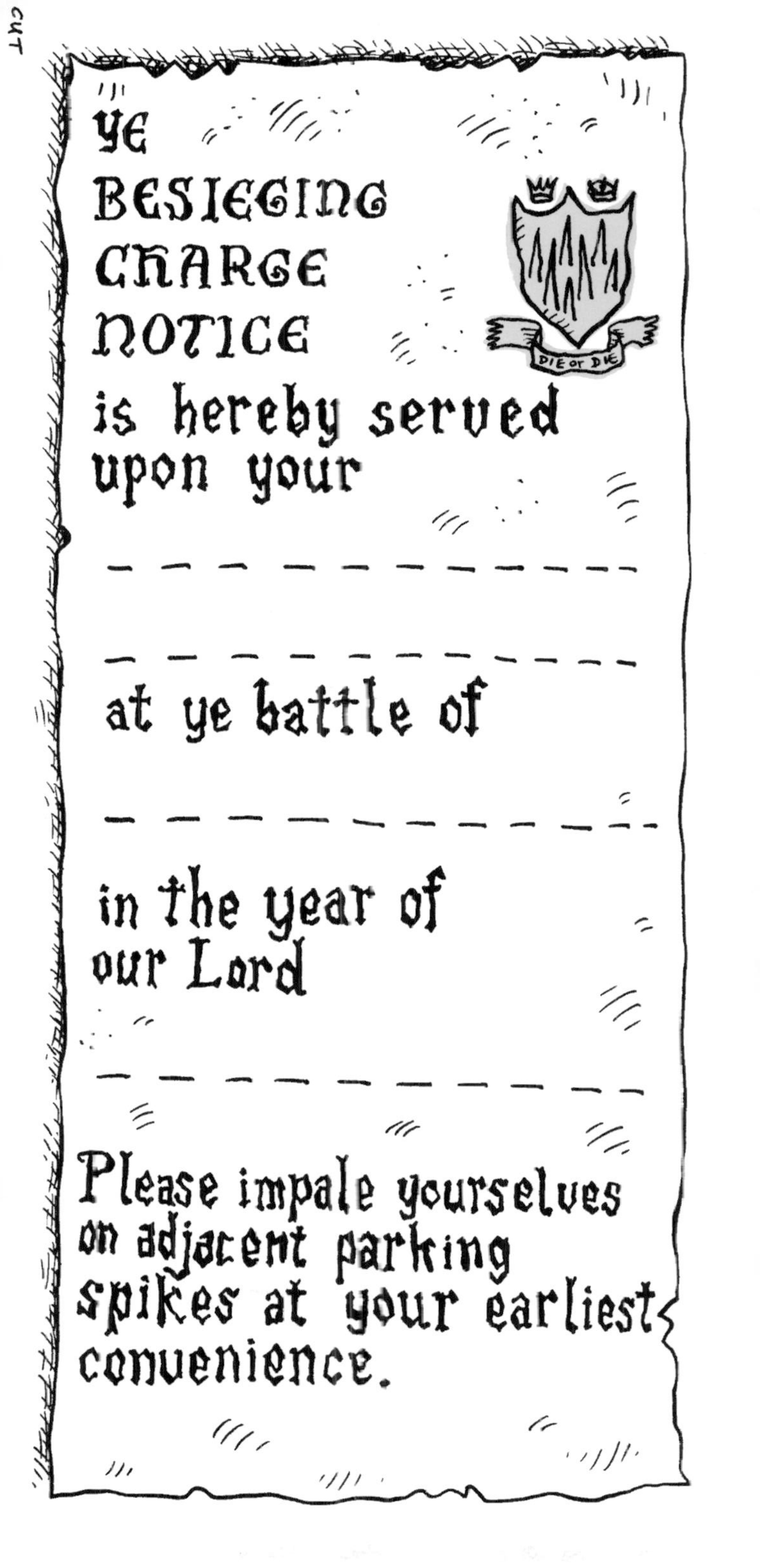

Ye

BESIEGING
CHARGE
NOTICE
is hereby served
upon your

at ye battle of

in the year of
our Lord

Please impale yourselves
on adjacent parking
spikes at your earliest
convenience.

DIE OR DIE

CUT

After that Napoleon tried to have Britain clamped and towed into the Atlantic. Nelson thwarted Napoleon's notice of removal by cutting the French clamp in Trafalgar Square. After Napoleon had escaped from Elba in a palindrome Wellington clamped a boot on him and parked him on a rock in St Helens. Throughout the rest of the nineteenth century Queen Victoria refused to acknowledge the existence of lesbians or parking.

The Golden Age of Parking Tickets dawned with the Rise of the Automobile. In the early days it was a privilege to own a car and a parking ticket was a sign of wealth. Maurice de Bindlestiffe writes in his memoir of motoring in Oxford, *Maurice Minor*, that: "In the early days a parking ticket was an occasion for celebration. The college parking warden, often another undergraduate, would dress in his official uniform, including velvet breeches and a wig, to deliver the ticket personally. The document would be served along with a dish of fresh muffins and a posset of mulled claret. Certain colleges produced their own tickets, illuminated by hand after the manner of William Morris."

OFF TO A TUTORIAL.

CARS LONGA METER BREVIS

*Trans: Your car has been here a long time, but there were only 15 minutes on the meter.

Translations also available in Sanskrit, Greek and Mediaeval French.

CUT

MODERN TIMES

By the 1960s parking meters had inspired popular songs and minor annoyance. As more and more of the common people were able to afford cars the police got fed up writing parking notices.

Finally everything in the UK was privatized and parking tickets were decriminalized. Now Britain is a proud leader in Parking Enforcement.

You're nicked, love.

JOHN LENNON

PARKING WARDEN OUTFITS DESIGNED BY MARY QUANT.

PHOTO BY DAVID BAILEY.

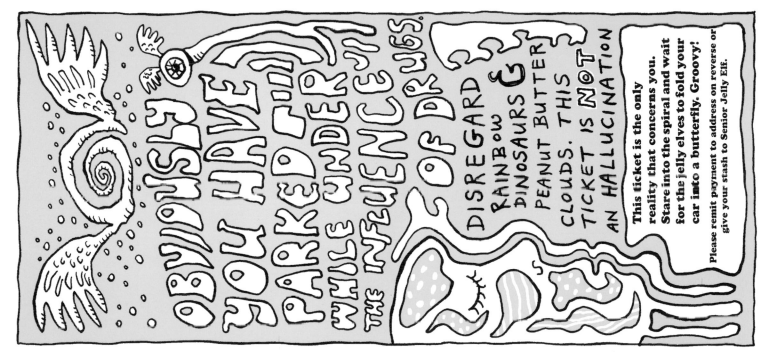

CUT

PARKING TICKETS IN OTHER LANDS & BEYOND

FRANCE

Across the Channel the parking ticket is also reviled. Paris suffers from acute *congestion de circulation*. With typical Gallic élan the parking authorities of the City of Lights have redesigned the uniforms of wardens, again. The previous designs by John Galliano were impractical: the crinolines prevented officers from reaching wind-screens or collecting money from meters. The new designs by Jean Paul Gaultier are very striking. Even the tickets have been redesigned, although there were some conceptual problems. The ticket pictured right, was highly controversial as it was pointed out that the artist Magritte was Belgian.

34

Alors! Votre voiture est merde.

IS THIS A TICKET? (SEE RIGHT)

REFRESHMENTS FOR THE WARDEN

There are several statutory excuses available to the French motorist:

Stationnement passionel – parking while engaged in adulterous relations is always permissible but the time period has been reduced to two hours.

Stationnement de dégustation – parking while eating in a three-star restaurant. The old days of the one-star, prix fixe, free parking are long gone.

Stationnement sportif – available to members of French national teams.

One of the strikers for the French World Cup team claimed to be having sex during a five-course lunch at *Le Chat Tordu* so he was allowed to park on the pavement in front of the restaurant for six days.

BELCH!

The European Court of Human Rights sent a delegation to protest the new French, language-free, tourist ticket (on right), but their minibus was clamped, towed away and pushed into the Seine.

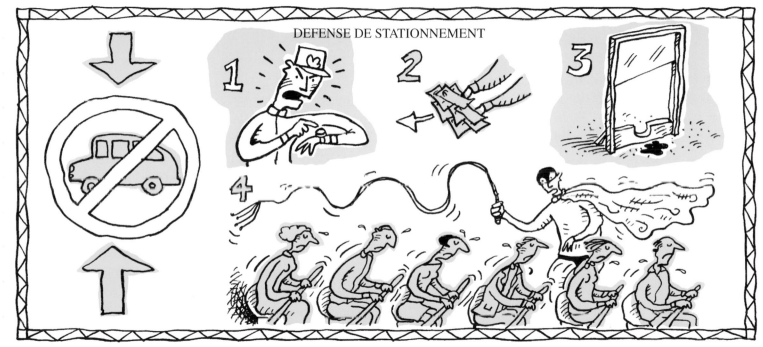

THE NETHERLANDS

Dutch wardens in the little town of Palingstad were so fed up with being objects of hatred and derision that they decided to reward motorists by leaving bunches of flowers on cars and offering massages.

ITALY

In Italy emotions run high and traffic cameras are regularly targeted by snipers. In Milano parking meters allow only fashionable cars to park. Unfashionable vehicles are towed away. On the other hand, in Bologna luxury cars and other vehicles of social oppression are awarded tickets. In Roma traffic is so bad that every car owner is sent fifty tickets every year regardless of whether they park or not.

Luckily Italian bureaucracy is so slow you may never receive a ticket in your lifetime but unfortunately under Italian law you can be forced to inherit parking tickets (see right).

R.I.P.

Reddito Italiano di Parcheggio

MULTA EREDITATTA
(INHERITED TICKET)

Questa multa was given to your
great, great, great grandmother
for leading a herd of goats on
the wrong side of the piazza,
la domenica, 13 agosto, 1843.

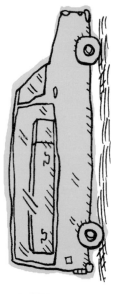

WITH INTEREST YOU
NOW OWE: € 37 millioni

CUT

JAPAN, CHINA & HAITI

Japanese wardens often dress up as manga figures to deflect anger, while in Beijing cars can be fined for 'unsuitable space placement'.

You're right. My chi is flowing properly again.

my pleasure.

Chinese parking control officers are trained in vehicular feng shui.

In Haiti the undead make excellent parking control officials. They only work at night but can be housed cheaply in existing crypts. Cars are cursed rather than clamped. It costs a certain amount to lift a curse but drivers always pay as no one has ever survived driving a damned vehicle. Drivers of cursed cars are sentenced to live their lives as snivelling, impotent shadows barely able to function, or they are doomed to be zombie wardens. It is hard to say which is a worse fate.

CUT

INDIA

In Jaipur, turbaned wardens patrol the streets with colourful elephants. These "Pink Parkyderms" sit on illegally parked vehicles until the fine is paid. If the fine is not paid then the elephant simply sits down a little harder. Baby elephants start their training by sitting on bicycles, moving up to mopeds and rickshaws. Wardens leave tickets translated into several languages or slide cobras through the passenger windows. On payment of fines the cobras are then charmed out of the vehicles. Many motorists leave a mongoose in the car in case of an Official Snaking. The wardens have now taken to tempting the mongeese out of cars using eggs.

THE UNITED STATES

American cities like Las Vegas, Nevada, and Atlantic City, New Jersey, feature Chance Parking. With a dollar slot meter you can win up to a month's parking or owe so much money that your car will be towed away and impounded. Sadly many gamblers become addicted to parking.

CUT

PARKING IN SPACE

The universe is severely congested with stars and other heavenly bodies. Some sort of control is needed. The Milky Way is jammed and even the smallest planet is lucky to find a spot.

Scientists believe the planets in our solar system have orbited our sun for many millions of years in search of parking. Saturn is still wearing a clamp from millions of years ago.

PARKING CONTROL SAVES THE EARTH

An alien invasion from Gnomos IV was thwarted by the parking system of the Greater London Council. On 23rd December attack drones landed and took up positions on major London streets. The invasion failed when the one-legged attack drones were overfed by Christmas shoppers.

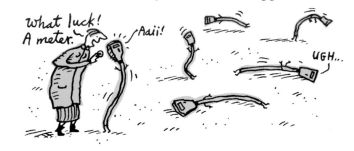

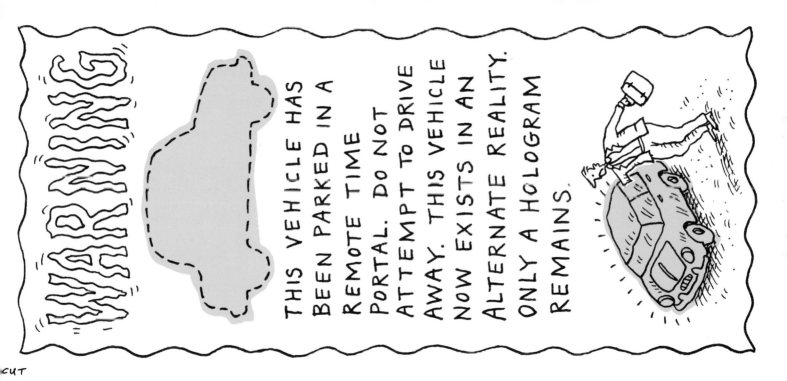

WARNING

THIS VEHICLE HAS BEEN PARKED IN A REMOTE TIME PORTAL. DO NOT ATTEMPT TO DRIVE AWAY. THIS VEHICLE NOW EXISTS IN AN ALTERNATE REALITY. ONLY A HOLOGRAM REMAINS.

CUT

An Interlude...

How To Talk Your Way Out Of A Parking Ticket

1. Reasonable explanation:

2. Weeping:

3. Begging:

4. Bribery:

5. Sex, offer of:

6. Death, just pretending:

How To Fail Miserably At Talking Your Way Out Of A Ticket

a. Legal action:

b. Threats:

c. Alien disguise:

d. Pathetic excuses:

e. Mirror:

f. Insanity:

Blee blee...

BE YOUR OWN WARDEN*

Now for some fun. Experience the thrill of leaving a parking ticket on a windscreen!

Some helpful tips:
– Ensure that the driver of the vehicle you wish to cite is neither in the vehicle nor close by.
– Consider working under cover of darkness or in a disguise.
– Once you have left the ticket retreat to a safe distance.
– Resist the temptation to laugh or call attention to yourself in any way.
– UNDER NO CIRCUMSTANCES CONFRONT OR RIDICULE DRIVER – unless driver is smaller than yourself and unarmed.

NOTE: try wearing the special badge (opposite). Some joker suggested pinning this on a real warden, which would be a really bad thing to do. But pretty hilarious. Of course, Messrs Mole & Appleby and their whosits and whatsits do not condone in any way blah blah blah (see previous page)...

fig a: fig b:

ARE PARKING TICKETS NECESSARY?

Of course not. It's all a vicious plot to drive us to the brink of insanity. But one does have to consider the selfish behaviour of other motorists. I mean, really, look how people park! Slap this on their windscreen to remind the buggers they can't just put it anywhere.

NOT A Parking Control Notice

This is NOT a parking ticket because this is NOT parking. This is just leaving your car in the street. This kind of behaviour is simply not acceptable. Do you own the road? Are you God?

Small print: You are a se fish, uncivilized sod unfit to enjoy the benefits of human society. If you understood the concept of shame or had any shred of decency then leaving your vehicle like this would never have crossed your mind. Is your life so important that you may trample of the rights and privileges of others? This is a rhetorical question, DO NOT attempt to answer it. Next time park your car decently, relatively near to the kerb and away from other vehicles, using only ONE (one) space or your car will be towed and crushed with you ir it, you amoral lout.

(If you have received this message in error, or if you are God, please save it and attach it to a vehicle that you consider to be improperly positioned.)

SHAME ON YOU

CUT

A parking ticket can also be used as a reminder or a reward. Experiments have proved that reinforcing positive behaviour can have better results than punishing negative actions.
The ticket opposite can also be used as an ironic indicator of incompetence.

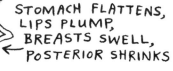

NOTICE HOW A POSITIVE PARKING CITATION WORKS LIKE A FACE-LIFT OR BOTOX

STOMACH FLATTENS, LIPS PLUMP, BREASTS SWELL, POSTERIOR SHRINKS

CUT

Some people just have no self-respect, much less any thought for their surroundings. Their vehicles are so unkempt it's offensive. This car is disgusting. It is not parked, it is littering the street. It should be picked up and put in a bin along with all the other rubbish. But let us be charitable, perhaps the owner is simply not aware. He or she just needs a kindly reminder.

SPOORS

HUGE MOLD FOREST

BIRD POO

MOSS

CRUSHED INSECTS

A DIRTY CAR

REVEALS A DIRTY, DISORGANIZED AND CHAOTIC MIND.

Wash your car and all aspects of your life – including love, finance and work – are guaranteed to improve.

(A gentle piece of encouragement from a helpful neighbour, so pay attention you filthy bastard.)

CUT

Parking doesn't hurt the environment, driving does. Once a car is parked the damage is done. Why not give driving tickets instead? The bigger the vehicle the bigger the ticket. Have you seen the size of some cars? Slap this on one of those belching behemoths and show Our Planet that you care.

DRIVING CONTROL OFFICERS GIVE DRIVING TICKETS TO MOVING VEHICLES.

OFFICIAL NOTIFICATION

OF EXCESSIVE SHOWING OFF

You have exceeded your ostentation allowance. Your inflated ego has become a strain on the resources of the earth. It is time to buy a smaller car, more in keeping with your station in life.

CUT

Perhaps you feel the pendulum has swung too far.
Why shouldn't you be allowed to drive whatever
you want? Do we live in a dictatorship?
Motorists! Your right to drive great, big,
inefficient cars is threatened! Fight back!
Stick this ticket on all small,
fuel-efficient cars or bicycles
in your area and show them
who's boss!

A TICKET FOR PEOPLE WITHOUT CARS

YOU SELF-RIGHTEOUS GIT!

If you think your pathetic protest against climate control is going to have any effect you are very much mistaken.

A: Go back to your commune and weave another goat-hair thong while cranking the generator for your recycled, sustainable-mahogany pleasure wand.

B: You're just jealous of people who can afford a decent car.

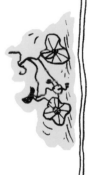

CUT

Should parking control be for profit? Do they have to gouge us at every turn? Certain London boroughs have given contracts to roaming bands of parking vigilantes. This is an exciting growth area as bands of self-righteous NIMBYs and eco-terrorists are happy to do the job for a fraction of the cost. Parking vigilantes hope that parking will be recriminalized. According to Don "the Luddite" Kirtelby, "Owning a car should be made a capital offence to safeguard the environment. Anyone found defiling the planet by driving or parking should be hanged, drawn and quartered. Their mutilated bodies should be put in a cage for all to see and their vile instrument of environmental destruction should be burned in an auto-da-fé. Power to the pedestrians!"

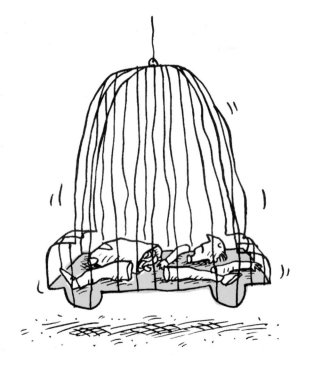

YOU HAVE BEEN FOUND GUILTY BY A JURY OF YOUR BETTERS OF OWNING A CAR.

THE SENTENCE IS **DEATH**.

YOU WILL BE TAKEN, BY BICYCLE, TO A PLACE WHERE YOU WILL SUFFER YOUR FATE.

MAY GOD HAVE MERCY ON YOUR SOUL, IF YOU HAVE ONE.

CUT

And why not include the whole family? Let the little ones write a few tickets, too. Another exciting innovation in the Parking Control Sector is the cadet training scheme inaugurated last year. Junior Wardens – children of primary school age – are sent out into the streets to spot parking violators. Bradbury Valentine, child exploitation consultant, says that child labour laws have been avoided by simply bribing participating local authorities. "Besides, the kiddies are only too happy to get out of school for the day and it's more fun than trainspotting. We even let the kiddies design their own tickets, which helps with their art and cuts down on costs."

Junior wardens ticket

Yur car is # poopy. It is a big pece of poo.

Don Park yur poopy car here agen.

My Dads car iz miles better than yor little poo car.

cut

How many times has a meter run out early? You put in half an hour and come back twenty-eight minutes later to a ticket. A big advantage of being a parking control officer is that time has no real meaning. Meters are set to run out early and most wardens are encouraged to play fast and loose with posted time limits.

In fact, the parking control day is only 22 hours long or 21.5 hours DST (daylight savings ticketing).

PARKING WARDEN's WATCH:

MIDDAY AT 10:00 AM

SOME HOURS SHORTER THAN OTHERS

NO TICK. SILENT FOR SNEAKING UP...

'7' MISSING ALTOGETHER

THURBLESDAY

LUCKY

• INCLUDES MADE-UP DAYS & LUCKY DAYS.
• HANDS WHICH MOVE AT VARIABLE SPEEDS.

RETROACTIVE PARKING TICKET

LAST WEEK YOU WERE PARKED ILLEGALLY.

YOU ARE BEING CHARGED IN ARREARS FOR A PREVIOUSLY COMMITTED OFFENCE.

Payment is therefore being increased by 17.65% to cover the interest charges.

Did I own a car last week?

CUT

Parking tickets can predict the future. Extrasensory Parking (ESP) is an exciting growth area for parking enforcement. Enjoy a feeling of security by taking care of a violation before it happens. And why not take advantage of the new Appleby & Mole breakdown services who will tow your car to a service station before it breaks down!

P.C.P.

(PARKING CONTROL PREDICTION)

Our psychic parking control officer has determined that you will commit an offence in the near future.

On Thursday of next week you will park illegally outside your mum's just for ten minutes while she tries to find her bag.

Early violation resolution! Pay now and save!

CUT

SEX & PARKING

Paradoxically, some find parking control highly arousing. The clamp may be seen as an instrument of bondage. Towing represents the threat of castration. Members of both sexes are attracted to the warden as a symbol of uniformed power. In fact, the traffic warden ranks number five in the fantasy sex-play character top ten.

Consider these highly suggestive phrases:

"I'm going to have to stick it under there."

"Go on, I dare you to give it to me."

"I'll only be inside for a couple of minutes."

"Don't do it or my husband will be furious."

"Please don't tell my wife you gave me one."

This is better than a ticket any day.

Thank you, warden.

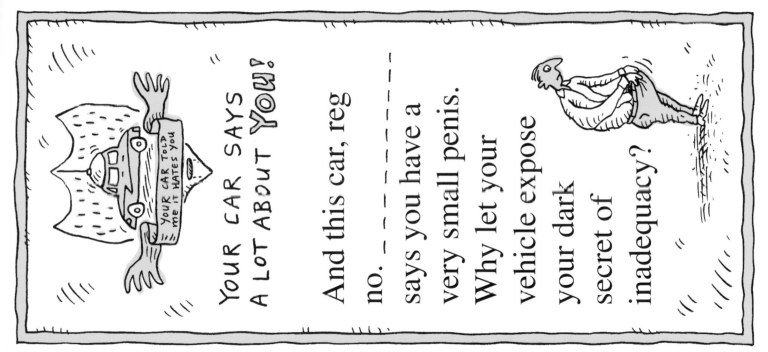

CUT

Stuck for a gift this holiday season? Send a violation notice as a Christmas card and save money. Go through a red light near a traffic camera and tell the family to get out of the car quickly and crouch down near the number plate.
Don't forget to SMILE!

Then do something nice for a strange car to help it impress and date lady cars. A random act of kindness to inanimate objects never goes amiss (see right). Uncertain of the sex of your vehicle? Check your owner's handbook or look closely at the undercarriage.

80

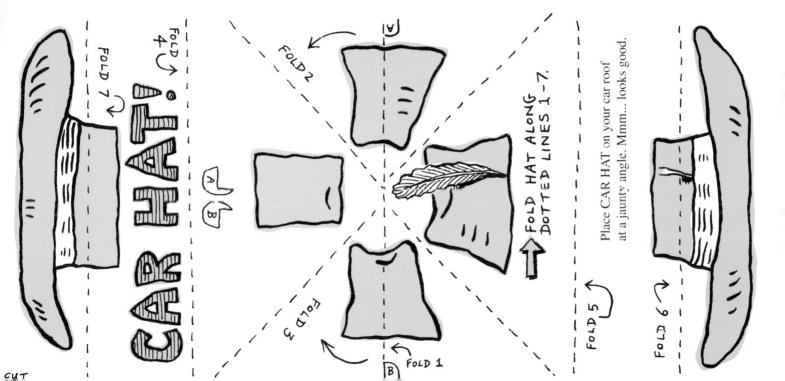

CAR HAT!

CUT

FOLD 4

FOLD 7

[A]

FOLD 2

[A] [B]

FOLD HAT ALONG DOTTED LINES 1-7.

FOLD 3

FOLD 1

[B]

Place CAR HAT on your car roof at a jaunty angle. Mmm... looks good.

FOLD 5

FOLD 6

PARKING: NEW APPROACHES & THE FUTURE

PUBLIC TRANSPORT

Oh, the humiliation!

Forced to sit cheek by jowl with the
unwashed multitude.

Press-ganged into pointless conversation
with strangers.

Waiting in the cold for the 49.

Cursing the 8.34, cancelled due to signal failure at
Fannington Hill.

Crammed into overheated carriages in a fog of
body odour.

Forced underground like vermin.

Flesh pressed against "Mind the Doors!" glass.

Souls crushed and dreams coarsened by a daily
dose of enforced advertising.

Before we consider such a drastic measure, let us
look at dynamic new approaches to parking. For
several years Parisians and New Yorkers have been
encouraged to park in the less popular galleries of
the Louvre and the Metropolitan. Parts of the
Hermitage in Moscow are heated entirely by car
exhaust. The Tate Modern would make an excellent parking structure. Cars would be carefully
labelled to avoid being confused with exhibits.

STILL LIFE with VEHICLE

Appleby & Mole, June 2007, UK

Materials: metal, rubber, glass, petroleum by-products, avian guano, various semi-masticated foodstuffs.

The inhabitants of this car are examples of early twenty-first century city dwellers. Their drab vehicle mirrors their depressing urban lives. It resembles a cage in which they are reduced to the status of tame rodents insulated from the dangers but also the pleasures of the outside world.

CUT

Other public buildings would make excellent parking structures. Consider pulling into the House of Lords, parking in Big Ben or the London Eye. Or how about driving onto the field at Lords during a Test?

How about parking in the sky? Fill your car with helium and let it float above the street. Or pull into a giant parking airship courtesy of Graf Parken. Park in Godlaming, land in Heidleberg.

The Nimbus Parking Company is experimenting with cloud parking, but Parking Control is ready to meet the challenge.

CUT.

Or enjoy one of many parking barges on the Thames. Water parking is already a success on the rivers of Europe.

Alternatively, how about bringing sports onto the streets? Referees are hated as much as parking wardens. Why not make parking control more palatable by dressing wardens as referees? Wardens would hand out red and yellow cards to offending motorists.

DO NOT MOVE THIS GOAL!

CLUNK!

THIS CAR HAS BEEN DESIGNATED AN OFFICIAL GOAL FOR THE EURO CUP STREET FOOTBALL.

OTHER USES YOUR CAR MAY BE PUT TO INCLUDE:

• GRAND STAND.

• HAMBURGER STALL.

• CHANGING ROOM.

• TEAM SHOWERS.

CUT

The European car industry has tackled the car problem with customary ingenuity. Nevertheless, large parcels of land will still be needed. The Isle of Wight is under a compulsory purchase order for the construction of a giant multi-storey car park. Cars will be taken onto the island by ferry and motorists will be put on trains to other parts of southern England. The Isle of Man will also become a parking haven while Scottish motorists will park on Skye or the Bass Rock.

Once every available square inch of land, water or air has been used up, the parking industry must consider the only alternatives left: space and the Fourth Dimension (see right).

CUT

The future of parking tickets is in doubt. The parking industry has noticed a decline in takings. Raising prices is only one answer. Parking tickets must be made more attractive: how about a parking ticket which includes a book token or a coupon for Mole & Appleby's Automotive Spa? Or perhaps a violation with dinner and a show?

A pilot programme in London's West End was discontinued as too many people were deliberately parking illegally so as to enjoy one of the many singing wardens. The wardens are currently on tour in New York, writing tickets on Broadway and singing to New York theatregoers.

CUT

THIS TICKET HAS BEEN BROUGHT TO YOU BY
WILLIAM SHAKESPEARE!

Come and see *The Tempest!*
Present this parking notice at the box office for 25% off!

Then enjoy a late supper at Coglioni's in the heart of the West End. Your appetizers and a glass of house wine are FREE!

But wait, there's more! Your ticket has been written by PCO Jackie Booné at 19.35 hrs. Wait while Jackie makes the rounds and he'll be back to regale you with a musical favourite of your choice OR one of several soliloquies!
(*Midsummer Night's Dream* not available October – February. *Twelfth Night* available only 17th November – 10th January).

This vehicle has **not paid** the congestion charge and will be subject to removal on the next occasion.

THANKS FOR SUPPORTING LIVE THEATRE!

EPILOGUE: ENLIGHTENMENT

You've experienced the horror of getting tickets, you've had the pleasure of giving tickets. You have now reached a point in your journey where you can deal with parking tickets without anger. Take a deep breath...

See the ticket.

Be one with the ticket.

Become the ticket.

YOU ARE THE TICKET!

See yourself on the windscreen.

Read yourself.

Know the reason you are there.

Become the violation.

Feel (the) fine.